NOW
YOU
SEE
HER

NOW YOU SEE HER

Lisa Karen Cox, Maggie Huculak, Raha Javanfar, Amy Nostbakken, Norah Sadava, and Cheyenne Scott

COACH HOUSE BOOKS, TORONTO

first edition

Canada Council for the Arts Conseil des Arts du Canada ONTARIO ARTS COUNCIL CONSEIL DES ARTS DE L'ONTARIO an Ontario government agency un organisme du gouvernement de l'Ontario Canada

Published with the generous assistance of the Canada Council for the Arts and the Ontario Arts Council. Coach House Books also acknowledges the support of the Government of Canada through the Canada Book Fund and the Government of Ontario through the Ontario Book Publishing Tax Credit.

LIBRARY AND ARCHIVES CANADA CATALOGUING IN PUBLICATION

Title: Now you see her / a play by Lisa Karen Cox, Maggie Huculak, Raha Javanfar, Amy Nostbakken, Norah Sadava, and Cheyenne Scott.
Names: Cox, Lisa Karen, author. | Huculak, Maggie, author. | Javanfar, Raha, author. | Nostbakken, Amy, author. | Sadava, Norah, author. | Scott, Cheyenne, author.
Identifiers: Canadiana (print) 20200157612 | Canadiana (ebook) 20200157620 | ISBN 9781552454046 (softcover) | ISBN 9781770566262 (EPUB) | ISBN 9781770566354 (PDF)
Classification: LCC PS8605.O93547 N69 2020 | DDC C812/.6—dc23

Now You See Her is available as an ebook: ISBN 978 1 77056 626 2 (EPUB) and ISBN 978 1 77056 635 4 (PDF)

Purchase of the print version of this book entitles you to a free digital copy. To claim your ebook of this title, please email sales@chbooks.com with proof of purchase. (Coach House Books reserves the right to terminate the free digital download offer at any time.)

Sometimes people try to destroy you, precisely because they recognize your power – not because they don't see it, but because they see it and they don't want it to exist.

– bell hooks

A Note from the Creators

by Amy Nostbakken and Norah Sadava

Now You See Her was first conceived in 2015 when a woman in her sixties approached us after a performance and said, 'I remember the day it happened: I turned a certain age and suddenly I became invisible.' This simple truth struck a chord. We couldn't shake the question: how does this happen?

The erasure of women has a long history. It is a reality that continues to reverberate across this seemingly progressive, pluralistic country. With this play, we wanted to listen to and present stories that normally never find a stage. To stand up on our chairs and scream about the millions of ways that women have been, and still are, silenced.

Once we began to research and cast the show, we knew it would have to be authored by all of us. Every woman's experience is personal and nuanced; we seem to disappear on many levels at the same time in different ways. So we set out to co-author a play with six women.

Attempting to build a platform from which multiple voices can speak in an honest and safe way is not easy. It's inspiring, beautiful, and a laugh riot, but it is also a major challenge. The construction relies on patience, sweat, love, rigour, and years of commitment from many people who are willing to take massive risks. Every collaborator devoted themselves completely to this challenge. Witnessing each artist bravely expose their truth in the creation of *Now You See Her* was a profound gift. We hope that in turn these truths will amplify voices left unheard and illuminate stories left unseen.

Performance History

Now You See Her was originally presented in co-production with Quote Unquote Collective, Nightwood Theatre, and Why Not Theatre at Buddies in Bad Times in Toronto, November 2018.

Directed by Amy Nostbakken and Norah Sadava
Created and performed by Lisa Karen Cox, Maggie Huculak, Raha Javanfar, Amy Nostbakken, Norah Sadava, and Cheyenne Scott

Choreography – Orian Michaeli
Composition – Amy Nostbakken
Dramaturgy – Lisa Codrington and Falen Johnson
Set, Prop, and Costume Design – Jung-Hye Kim
Assistant Costume Design and Head of Wardrobe – Sim Suzer
Head of Props – Kira Duff
Lighting Design – André du Toit
Video Design – Kaitlin Hickey and Lily Ross-Millard
Sound Design – James Bunton
Additional Composition – Motion, DJ L'Oqenz, and Raha Javanfar
Creative Contributors – Émilie Monnet and Natasha Mumba

Production Manager – Suzie Balogh
Technical Director – Adrien Whan
Stage Manager – Tara Mohan
Assistant Stage Manager – Emily Maxwell
Live Sound Engineer – Amy Fort

www.quoteunquotecollective.com

Notes on Performance

Movement

The performance style in *Now You See Her* shifts between two worlds: individual characters in their own environments and the more abstract, highly choreographed chorus pieces.

Each character's movement style is based on an understanding of that woman's history, the layers of visibility and invisibility she deals with in her life. While she is inhabiting a naturalistic world, the chorus manifests her inner state through physical patterns and attitudes that contrast, colour, and contextualize. The chorus becomes Jennie's anxiety and her loneliness or Joanne's internal army of strength. The ensemble also fulfills more literal roles: Flo's backup dancers, Dez's girlfriend, or Kate's colleagues at a conference.

The play is structured around the four seasons, beginning in spring, moving through summer, fall, and winter, and coming back around to spring. Each season contains an ensemble piece correlating to a different phase in a woman's life. Spring is a dance of birth, summer breathes sex, autumn rages in hot flashes against the inevitable fall, and winter is death.

Orian Michaeli's group dances present women moving together in harmony to create a vision of a natural cycle. But outside impositions (violence, erasure, dismissal) cause damage to the natural order of things. When we return to spring at the end of the play, it's all fucked up. Twisted and warped. One woman has been erased, and her disappearance destroys the group and the cycle. We are in chaos. It's clear that we cannot proceed like this. The audience is left with the question: what needs to be done to make women visible?

Music

In this play we use music as much as text to tell the story. This includes both live and recorded arrangements, acoustic and electric instruments, sound bites, samples, voice manipulation, vocoders, drum machines, and a-cappella song.

The musical narrative follows the four seasons. We open in spring: staccato voice and plucked violin. Summer is a syrupy moan-song and drum beats. Fall is vocoder with synthetic techno rhythm. Winter is the wind. Like the movement, the a-cappella voice of the chorus is another tool to express the inner workings of a character. Kate's suppressed rage becomes a stretched-out howl, Jennie's claustrophobia is an anxious song cycle on loop, Joanne's self-doubt is the rhythmic breath of the chorus behind her. Flo's story is set on a concert tour, so this character's life is most often expressed through her songs and how she sings them.

Notes on Performance Style

The performance style of the play, in line with its characters, is extremely varied. Each woman inhabits her own distinct world. Kate is highly expressive and humorous, while Jennie exists in a silent, screen-based universe. Flo lives in the hypermasked, hypersexualized world of pop music, which is dismantled in her third act. Dez is a bubbling ball of energy who confides in the audience unabashedly. Joanne is a blunt, incisive writer who articulates her ideas with the wit of her pen. All women speak straight to the audience; their address is honest, truthful, and direct.

Darya inhabits her own particular universe. The narrator, the fool, the liberated woman (a myth), she sits outside the story, outside (his)tory, and she comments upon it all in heightened poetic text. She is able to move around the theatre without boundaries, free to see the other characters, to watch their scenes, to acknowledge the present moment, to touch the walls of the building, and to play with the audience's expectations. Darya should be performed without restraint. Like a wild animal, she is unpredictable and can turn on a dime.

The unifying performative style is one of rigour, muscle, and precision. Every look, every breath, every note, is decisive and loaded with meaning. The physical and vocal commitment to every moment onstage is a political act. Hear us. See us. We will not disappear.

Characters

Joanne: Commanding, sixty-four-year-old woman living in the Annex in Toronto. An undercover journalist, she has a thirty-five-year-old daughter who lives in Regina. The play opens on Joanne preparing to receive a lifetime achievement award in journalism.

Florence (Flo): Striking, fierce, French-Canadian, Black singer living in Montréal. She has two young kids. Florence is at the height of her career as a touring artist. We see two sides of her that are remarkably different: the onstage presence (Flo) and the offstage (Florence). We see a third layer when the actress drops the character and speaks, out of role, directly to the audience.

Dez: Spirited eighteen-year-old Saanich woman from the Straits Salish region of Vancouver Island, BC. Dez is transitioning from high school to university and trying to find where she fits in.

Katherine (Kate): Highly enthusiastic microbiologist, living in Halifax. Kate becomes increasingly pregnant through the first three-quarters of the play. She has to decide whether to keep the baby or travel to Brazil to complete her research, which would result in a ground-breaking study published in her name.

Jennie: New mother experiencing postpartum difficulties revolving around her body, losing the baby weight, and the general trials of new motherhood living in Edmonton. Over-exhausted and falling into a black hole of neuroses, we meet Jennie when she is fluctuating between an intense love for her baby and questioning her decision to have children at all.

Darya: A liberated woman. Free from the confines of the patriarchy. Thus a mythical creature. Darya is the storyteller/ageless observer who watches and comments as the narratives unfold. **Note:** All performers shift from playing a character to a nameless woman. During the choreographies they are not bound by the confines of their character but act out a freer 'all-woman.' Often the role of these 'all-women' is to work together. Sometimes it is to do the opposite.

Setting

The stage is bare except for a white floor, a white scrim, and a white upright piano.

Act 1, Scene 1
Spring

Darkness. DARYA is sitting on the top ledge of the piano with her violin, plucking it and looping the sound until a soundscape of raindrops is created. She continues to play and loop as the rain gets heavier. Lights slowly dawn on the rest of the women who are onstage wearing nude shifts under fur coats. They sit with their legs spread as if preparing to give birth. The spring choreography begins with slow, sparse movement alluding to birth – both literally and metaphorically as the birth of spring/nature/humanity. The choreography becomes increasingly violent, and the women shed their coats, as contractions and labour occur. The title 'SPRING' is projected on the scrim with imagery of a woman's back in movement. Darya joins the others in the dance and the violin-rain subsides as a vocal soundscape emerges. FLO removes the coats that have been shed, Darya climbs a ladder and pulls a cord that unleashes rain across the front of the stage, a baby is passed between three of them, then they all join each other in the heat of contractions. The grunting and pushing intensifies until on the final exhale they are sent upstage right where they will sit. Darya has wrapped the baby and hands it to JENNIE. Darya walks downstage to deliver her text. During this text DEZ is dancing full throttle around Darya – it's like a duet but Dez can't see Darya.

DARYA: Wakey wakey, everybody!
It's time! Yup, today, right now. This hour.
It's that time! Yeah! And we're here, and it's not by accident, am I right?
Don't blink (*hissing sound effect plays*). Or you'll miss four seasons passing by
for one night only
you will see,
or maybe you won't

or maybe you will
(*points to an audience member*) You ... might not.
These ordinary women ... vanish (*whoosh*) ... before your very eyes.
But for NOW. YOU. SEE –

Act 1, Scene 2
Dez

Dez is downstage right. She interrupts Darya and continues dancing.

DEZ: 'Heyyyy! Long hair, long hair. Heeeyyy! Don't care, don't care. Heeyyyy! If ain't nobody likin' what we doin' what we tell them, man, shit: Long hair don't care.'

I just got home from the most amazing bush party. So I'm sitting at the bonfire and then I hear someone playing a really bad version of 'Stairway to Heaven.' So I go to check it out. And I'm like holy shit, this is the most beautiful person I've ever seen. And I'm full-on entranced by this horrible, horrible 'Stairway to Heaven.' Her name is Michelle and she lives up-island on the Cowichan reserve. She's planning on going to UBC next year. That's insane, 'cause I want to go there too, for Environmental Sciences. I'll probably get in ... yeah, okay, my grades are kinda crappy, but it's not a big deal. I just have to pass my final exams.

At least History's easy. All I have to do is drop names like John A. Macdonald and Duncan Campbell Scott, and I'll get an A for sure. 'Cause, you know ... white guilt. Don't worry, I can say that. I'm part white.

Michelle gets it. Tonight we were connecting on another level. We were lying on the grass and I was like, 'So yeah ... the stars are pretty crazy. There's the Big Dipper. And the Little Dipper. And some other ones.' She's laughing – oh my God, she's leaning in. I should kiss her. Should I kiss her? Should I kiss her?

Dez starts dancing again. Her phone buzzes from the floor downstage.

Hold on.

She moves to her phone, checks who it is.

Ahhhhhhh, it's Michelle!!! 'Long hair don't care no shampoo.' I should text her something in my language. I'll use my app. I know, I know, I need to use an app, sorry.

(*On phone*) Okay, what do we got on this thing. *The deer is far, that's a big squirrel, do you like fruit? I like you* – oooooh. Too forward? Should I?

NE SṮI EṮ NEȻE.

She doesn't even speak SENĆOŦEN, she's not gonna know what it means. I'm doing it.

She hits 'send.' Darya enters from offstage, Dez falls back, Darya catches her and lifts her back up to standing, in a new state.

In this world they call me Dez and I'm Straits Salish of the Saanich Nation. Now that we've clarified that, I'm sure you can guess what happens to me in the end. That's fucked up. I'm tired of dying every night to make others feel something. I don't want to do it anymore. But I guess I signed up for this. So I'm going to speak with you in a way that is healthy for me, for my family, and hopefully for the other Indigenous women here.

ÍY, ȻNES QENOṈE HÁLE ṮÁ,. U, EUQ ȻNES QENOṈE HÁLE.

(*Translating*) It's good to see you all again. I never see you all.

Act 1, Scene 3
Kate's Conference 1

Lights snap to fill the stage and loud music is blasted. All of the women walk efficiently through the space with an air of importance. KATE sits upstage left to put her heels on. Kate gets up on her feet, walking tenuously and shakily like a baby deer finding its legs. Kate moves in a diagonal line at a slower rhythm than the rest. The moment she lands downstage right, the others have grouped around the piano upstage left. JOANNE sits at the piano, prepared to play.

KATE: So I'm at a four-day Synergy in Science conference here in Halifax.

Joanne begins playing Vivaldi's 'Spring.'

I'm a featured speaker tonight. I'm here to deliver my paper on the effects of multiple biological stressors on the honey bee colonies in South America. We've discovered that the presence of varroa mites and the presence of microsporidia parasites may be causing a synergistic interaction resulting in higher rates of colony collapse, so, you know, fascinating stuff. Anyway, I'm standing in a circle of colleagues having a conversation with Brian Levine, a brilliant bioengineer, when I feel a man's hand. Land. On my arm.

She places her left hand on her right arm. Stops, looks at hand.

And I feel it before I see who it belongs to and (*looks at guy*) yeah, I don't know this guy, and he's leaning in as though he's about to introduce himself but instead he speaks across me to Brian.

Beat, looks at arm, looks at guy, then Brian.

So, he's talking to Brian, they're talking about ... right, soybeans, crop doubling in Regina. (*Smiling and nodding.*) They're having a nice conversation and he's leaning right in like he's gonna tell me who he is.

Points to his name tag.

I can see that his name is Robert, so Robert and Brian, I gather, went to King's College together. His face is now right up close to my face.

Hand still on arm, she looks at it, looks at Robert, looks at Brian.

I can see he's got a mild case of eczema. He's still holding my arm and it's getting very heavy now, it's sweaty.

She looks around, and the chorus of women begins to sing.

There's probably ten types of bacteria growing under there. And I'm looking around, trying to find somebody to make eye contact with. And I wonder ....

All women including Kate howl in a dissonant chord: 'How. Long.'

How long ... I'm going to be waiting.

Act 1, Scene 4
Joanne

A recording of Kate's final 'waiting' is heard echoing and growing, then morphing into Joanne's voice repeating the same word. Kate turns upstage and meets Joanne, who is crossing diagonally downstage; they see each other and have a brief moment of connection. Joanne starts to melt. At first Kate moves out of her way and watches her. Just as she is about to fall, the sound of a telephone echoes in the distance. Kate catches her and sends her downstage centre.

JOANNE: I am waiting for my heart to stop pounding ... I just got off the phone with the CJF, who called to tell me that I've been given the honour of a Canadian Journalism Foundation lifetime achievement award.

Turns back as if to look at phone.

They said, and I quote, that 'my commitment to journalism and social activism over four decades embodies what a lifetime of journalism should be.'

All the women file onto the stage in military formation and form a 'V' behind Joanne. Jennie's baby cries; she shushes it and runs to sit on the piano bench, calming the baby.

I will be receiving this award in the autumn in Toronto. (*Beat*) So.

The chorus of women perform precise, militant choreography, emphasizing Joanne's text. With each movement, there is a sharp inhale or exhale of breath. They are learning from Joanne, reinforcing her; they are her internal battalion preparing her for war.

That gives me six months to figure out what I'm going to wear. I'm not going to wear pants. At my age, with this face, I'll look like a man. I gotta wear a dress. But I can't wear my perfect sleeveless anymore because of these.

Jiggles right tricep.

Ah! I do have an okay dress with a low neckline that features my décolletage – but I have no cleavage. And now there's this lump here. And yes, I got it checked out – it's not cancer, it's just ugly. Ah! I have a dress with a higher neckline … but it's short, and there's these.

Lifts her shift and jiggles the flesh above her knees.

I could wear stockings to lift. That means high heels. Did you know that as you age, the collagen in your feet disappears and you are ostensibly walking on bone? That's okay. They make jelly insoles. Okay, so, no wheat, no sugar, no dairy, no caffeine, no booze. I can do that. Over Thanksgiving. Fuck. (*Beat*) But it's true, two years ago I quit drinking for six months and every person I ran into said, 'Oh my God, Joanne, what did you do, you look amazing!' I would *never* get a facelift. Well, maybe just a little one here, over the eyes. I mean, I can hardly *see* anymore. I gotta get rid of my hunch. Oh! And that short dress is dark, so if I have a hot flash, no one will see my sweat.

Act 1, Scene 5
Flo's Clock

The stage goes dark, Flo's drum beat starts, along with sounds of a crowd screaming. A pump-up countdown video plays, taking over the entire back scrim: clips of neon city lights, glam, Flo in various costumes, money, fur, cars, animal prints ... In the darkness the women leave the stage. Flo walks in front of the video with a cordless mic. Her handler (Kate) enters and hands Flo some chains/shackles to put on. Flo reasons with the handler that they will be too heavy and noisy. They have a small disagreement interrupted mid-sentence by:

FLO: Hello, San Francisco! ARE ... YOU ... READY?!

Flo takes the chains and, with her handler's help, puts them on while speaking. She exits.

Act 1, Scene 6
Jennie Googles

Jennie enters with her laptop and cellphone. A recording of Flo's pop song plays underneath this scene from the radio on her phone. A recording of radio announcers introduces the song:

VOICE 1: *So everyone's favourite diva, Flo, threw a tantrum before a concert in San Francisco on Saturday. (Cat sound effect)*

VOICE 2: *Yikes, cat fight!*

VOICE 1: *Sources say she downright refused to wear a silver costume piece crafted by world-famous designer Yves St. Laurent.*

VOICE 2: *Ouch, angry much?*

VOICE 1: *But here's her number one hit single ... (trails off into her song).*

Jennie opens her laptop; screen is projected on scrim. Her Facebook page is open and her profile photo is of her baby. A racist cartoon mocking Flo's 'freakout' about not wearing chains appears as a pop-up on her screen.

She closes it and googles:

Pregnant celebrities before & after (images)
How long to lose baby weight?
What if I hate being a mom?

She scrolls through some searches and settles on one article after another. Throughout, pop-up ads crop up with pornographic/suggestive/sexualized imagery.

The baby cries offstage and Jennie exits; she leaves the laptop open and a 'virus' overtakes the screen. Images of women's stomachs flash in succession, starting with just a few sporadic images until they overlap at a manic speed throughout the rest of the scene. Jennie re-enters, walking and humming to her baby, trying to put it to sleep. As the projection continues, all the other women walk around the stage; they are new mothers at home, moving through space in a zombie-like mode – underslept and understimulated. As they move, Jennie begins to undress them, one by one taking off their slips as if helping a child undress. As they move, they sing a six-part harmony, different melodic lines that layer on top of each other to create an anxious loop. Gradually the melody builds and Jennie's pace quickens until she's stripped all the women into their bras and underwear. The speed she moves is manic and the singing reaches a chaotic apex. As the women trickle offstage, the singing stops and the images disappear. Jennie pauses and checks the baby. Finding it asleep, she carefully creates a nest with the abandoned slips and gently leaves the baby in it to sleep. Everything is hushed. Relieved, she silently moves to exit upstage right, but the chorus abruptly belts out the melody again, returning to the stage. The baby is crying, there is no rest. Jennie returns to pick up the baby and exits, frustrated and alone.

Act 1, Scene 7
Women Get the Vote

From the catwalk stage left, Darya joins the melody of voices with her viola. The singing fades out and the violin version turns into a brief angry solo. Kate plays the music/sound effects that underscore this scene using a drum machine from onstage.

DARYA: Look up, look waaay up. Hey guys, how ya doin'? I got a question for ya:
Who? Little Cindy-Lou, who are the ladies we have to crane our necks to see
In this robustly hipped country? (*Purr*) Who, Betty Boo, who? 1927. (*Jingle*)
Famous five fought for the female vote. Whoa, Nellie McClung, the only one
Anyone
Remembers by name.
A woman is a person now and all persons can vote. 1927. Note.
It. That. They said whoa, whoa, Nellie, whoa, slow down, horsey, strap the feed bag back on until 1929, so 1929, damn, ninety years feelin' fine, shit fuck damn no not
So fine sugar
In Quebec.
Where women could not vote until 1940, note:
How fucked that is.
So not 1929, but 1940. No, no, slow down the train, 'cause the tracks ain't built. Chinese and Indian women could not vote, Debbie Downer, so not 1929 or '40 but '47, WAIT.

Music enters.

If you please.
For us to strip the civil rights and smack the hard-ass label
'enemy aliens' over the mouths of the Japanese.
Who did not, would not, 'cause could not vote until 1949.
I know you're trying
to keep up and you can prob'ly see what's coming 'cause the
tundra's pulse is drumming and the Inuit did not hold the right
to vote on shite that did not mean a thing to them until
1960
and there were no ballot boxes so far north so really
you can't actually say dick
Slow down!

Music exits.

'Cause I am wearing heels
and I can't run for shit
But okay,
okay yes, okay, chatty Kathy, can we now safely say
that by 1960 WOMEN.
Held in by an imaginary line
Divided and defined (*Hit*)
Divided and defined (*Hit*) (*Hit*) (*Lion growl*)
Divided and defined
By a band of white man's hands
Could place votes
As persons?

Darya laughs and leaves the mic, her laughter echoes until she gestures for it to stop. (Cougar growl)

In your dreams,
Scott Free.

Not
until 1969. (*Music enters*)
The year a gang of white men banged our silver moon, the self-same one we've held in our wombs, were Indigenous women allowed.
Yeah, with the RIGHT ID.
And the RIGHT address.
Yeah, in 1969 (in this country), all women held tight
with their teeth
to our right.
To take one small step
For man.

Act 2, Scene 1
Summer

A recording plays with music and the following text: 'There was a time when beaver lodges like this one, and the busy beaver that builds them, almost disappeared from Canada, because of overtrapping. But the beaver, who will always be associated with Canada's early days, has been reintroduced into many areas and has made a successful comeback.'

During this recording, Flo enters, stands behind Kate, and stuffs her belly to appear pregnant. The summer projection appears: the word 'SUMMER' and an image of a woman's neck and collarbone, skin and sweat. The women, who have all changed into summer costumes, enter and take their places, scattered across the stage, lying on the floor on their stomachs. They start humming as the beaver recording fades away. The summer choreography begins slowly and languidly, like molasses. They are masturbating. Halfway through, we hear the baby cry offstage and Jennie has to leave. As the music and movement heat up, the beat drops and the women exude electrified pleasure and playfulness. They embody the freedom and looseness of the summer, and the joy of sex and self-pleasuring.

Act 2, Scene 2
Kate's Conference 2

Kate stands up, putting on her glasses. She speaks just as the apex of the summer choreography (orgasm) climaxes around her.

KATE: So, I'm at the third annual conference on Biotic Change, here to announce that we have indeed secured funding and will be leaving for Brazil in just under four months, so let the countdown begin!

The summer dance ends. Joanne is at the piano playing a lame-ass version of 'Summer in the City.' The other women exit, Kate takes a canape from one of their hands as they pass.

Barry and Tim are here from the National Agricultural Statistics Association and David from the University of Maryland, who is a specialist on varroa mites, is explaining how he was forced to stop calling the women in his office 'girls,' and I wish Tim would get back to talking about the winter losses for colony collapse ...

To Tim at her right:

Yeah, so, Tim ...

To Barry, at her left:

Well, actually, according to ...

Back to Tim:

Yes, actually, my team and I went to ... Yep, well, Tim, I'd like to hear more about ... My team and I actually ... I agree it's harkening back to the files ... California ...

... Sorry, but really I think that you'll find that ... Yep, all right.

Colony collapse disorder is the phenomenon that occurs when the majority of worker bees in a colony take off and abandon the queen.

I wonder if I just stop talking ...

Flo enters and starts to walk downstage.

... when they'll notice that I'm not saying anything.

Act 2, Scene 3
Never Ever

FLO: Never. No never ...

One by one, the women enter quickly, move into a line downstage, and speak to the audience in unison rhythmically and in pitch.

ALL WOMEN: ... could I ever, baby, no never ever, baby, EVER be the president. 'Cause once a month, of course. Quarter of my life, coursing through my insides, I'm struck with my curse.

The baby cries and Jennie walks offstage. At this point, blood starts drooling down the legs of Darya, then Flo, then Dez. Jennie re-enters to try to shush the women, sees the blood on the floor, and proceeds to clean it up with rags.

I'm fucked! With the best and the worst possible punishment for being born. This way.

Grabs crotch, stomach, breasts.

ALL WOMEN: And of course, when that time, when MY time rolls around to pick me up in her red Corvette, I jump IN with Sister Hysteria and we (of course) will be driven to push the big red button and drop the A BOMB ... That's what will happen! You know it! I know it! ... On Japan! Again!

All the women leave the stage. Kate has been looking down at the other women's blood, then at her own crotch. Joanne looks at Kate.

JOANNE: You're pregnant.

Act 2, Scene 4
Tracing

Darya and Dez enter in a game of chase around Kate and Joanne as they exit, then abruptly meet downstage left and begin a choreography of tracing/exploring each other's body with their fingertips. Just as Kate is about to exit, Jennie meets her and these two women perform the exact same tracing duet as Darya and Dez.

DEZ: Michelle's visiting me for the whole weekend. I went and picked some blackberries, or SꝀELÁLN̲EW̲, for this special occasion. The bees were terrorizing me but I was like a ninja in the bush and evaded them. Bees are cool, just, like, don't be rude.

I've brought Michelle to my favourite place. My grandfather made that bench. Sometimes I like to skip stones, but when the tide is out I kick over the big rocks and watch the baby crabs scramble for cover. I know, I know. Rude. I'm going to miss this place, I think. But I'm glad Michelle gets to see it before I leave. You know how she loves classic rock, right? Well, Mom and Dad always played Pink Floyd's *The Dark Side of the Moon* on road trips. It was the one CD in our truck. I'm obsessed with that song, 'Great Gig in the Sky.' My dad told me the girl who sings on that song, Clare Torry, totally improvised that insane vocal track in, like, one take, and then Pink Floyd didn't even credit her. They were like, 'Yeah, all right, whateva'. She didn't even know she was on the album until she bought a copy. Yeah. Michelle is totally impressed with my music suave right now.

She wants to be a lawyer and is always talking about Sharon McIvor, Dr. Pam Palmater, and Mary Two-Axe Earley. I had to google who they were while she was talking. The only famous Native women I know about are Tanya

Tagaq and Buffy Sainte-Marie. I guess I'm a shitty Native. First Nations. Indigenous person.

Michelle knows exactly what she wants in life and is so confident. (*Smiles*) She asked me if I wanted to live with her in Vancouver in the fall. I said yes, obviously. Mom and Dad aren't super convinced. Mom's worried about transit. But that's just part of living in the city.

Last night, though, Mom came into my room with one of those zipper fabric protector thingies and she was like, 'I know I've been emotional lately, and it's just because I worry,' and she unzipped the thingy and pulled out a beautiful fur coat. It was my grandmother's. She passed it on to my mother, and Mom gave it to me to take to the city.

Act 2, Scene 5
Flo's Pop Song

We hear a recording of Flo's beat. Jennie runs to the front of the audience and hands her baby to an audience member saying, 'I can't do the next thing while holding her. Would you mind?' Flo does an impressive choreographed dance throughout this song, with the rest of the women joining in as backup dancers behind her.

FLO: (*Sung*) Move to the side when we step up in the club
buying out the bar
get the DJ run the dub
run the riddim, fill the floor
getting points off the door
always plotting, planning, cashing,
getting focused, getting more

I been poppin bottles, poppin cherries, poppin champagne
Betta pull over, or you crash in my fast lane
If you copped a Maserati, couldn't catch me
You wanna twin me, bitch you couldn't match me

A wah do dem
a wah do dem dem dem
me nah really really up inna de
friend friend ting

Too many gyal inna de i-diot ting
wan fight ovah man
but him nah give me nothing

I run dollahs, run biz, run tings
On top of the world and hella things the gwop brings

Don't look at me funny
Can't shade me, don't judge me
Young, hot, and ready with a bank fulla money

Me nah play
Me nah joke
Me nah ramp

Cause it's my life
It's not a game
Me nah ramp

Cause it's my life
Get out my way
While my wild women slay
Me nah skin
Me na grin –

The music stops abruptly, and Flo turns around looking up to the tech booth. The dancers start to stretch and take drinks of water, abandoning Flo with their silence. We realize this has been a rehearsal. Flo reacts as though her manager is speaking to her from the booth.

FLO: What's up, Jimmy?

Pause, listening.

Oh, well ... I can't sing at that part because I'm totally winded. I mean, I can't sing well and do that move at the same time. I figure there's a track playing and I can do that move way better with the mic down.

Pause, listening.

I totally appreciate that you are trying to ... honour my West Indian heritage but I'm not sure we do that with that particular dance move ... Plus, they're all ... not from the Caribbean ...

Pause, listening.

I'm not suggesting we change it. I just ... I can't breathe ...

Pauses, listening. Then recovers.

No, I hear ya. Loud and clear. Where would you like to go from?

To her backup dancers:

Sorry about that, ladies. Thanks for your patience.

Flo and the dancers get into position.

FLO: (*Yelling*) BANK FULL OF MONEY

The music kicks back in.

Me nah play
Me nah joke
Me nah ramp

Cause it's my life
It's not a game
Me nah ramp

Cause it's my life
Get out my way
While my wild women slay

me nah skin
me nah grin
Me nah ramp

Me nah play
Me nah joke
Me nah ramp

Cause it's my life
It's not a game
Me nah ramp

Cause it's my life
Get out my way
While my wild women slay
me nah skin
me nah grin
Me nah ramp

Morning in the interviews
afternoon I model
Evening in the studios
midnite with my bottles
and my bitches, and the groupies
in the club, VIP
while you staring at the screen
Pressing like on IG

I'm a new blood with vet status
started rapping – then star-grabbing
my chart action
cash stacking
Red carpets is flashing
lifestyles of the 'hood rich and high fashion

I got music for the cars and the strip bars
For the Grammys, AMAs, and the Billboard
for the 'hood, Wall Street, and the yacht club
everybody wan' live what the block does

Freak in sheets
Gangsta in the streets
Lady in the limo
with the heat under the seat

Still a street chick, mean bitch
sick bitch, rich bitch
A made bitch, brave switchblade not-afraid bitch

So put 'em up! Give me all your money
I'm a boss bitch, gimme all your money
I'm your boss bitch, taking all your money
Ladies put 'em up if you're making your own money

Loud women
Proud women
Sound women
Down women
Upping up the vibe women
Raise 'em to the sky wid 'em

Loud women
Proud women
Sound women
Down women
Upping up the vibe
Raise 'em to the sky

Me nah play
Me nah joke
Me nah ramp

Cause it's my life
It's not a game
Me nah ramp

Cause it's my life
Get out my way
While all my wild women slay
me nah skin
me nah grin
Me nah ramp

Cause it's my life
Can't stop my element
It's my life
Can't stop my relevance

Never
I'm a queen bitch
Lioness
doing it
supplying it
You're trying it
And haters still buying it.

Flo does one final look back to the audience and the lights go to black; we hear her breathing on mic in the dark.

Act 2, Scene 6
Walking in the Night

We are in complete darkness. Flo continues to breathe. The other women enter when they speak their first lines. Each woman is carrying a cell phone that she turns on to illuminate her face as she speaks, until all six women are illuminated. In a choreography of panic and fear, they move around the whole stage and up into the aisles of the audience. Sometimes they all stop simultaneously; sometimes only one runs around; sometimes they all run. Sometimes they move in a pattern; other times, it is chaos.

JOANNE: I used to avoid a stretch of Osler – that whole strip north of College, east of Broad, by the hospital.

DEZ: If I don't take the bus at the corner of Hastings and Cambie, then I have to go all the way back up to the Skytrain and transfer to another bus.

KATE: When I get off work it's about three in the morning. Some of the girls hold their keys, but I just carry my money belt over my shoulder.

DEZ: And while I wait for the bus in the pitch-dark I'm thinking: I am so stupid.

KATE: There are so many coins in there I figure I could knock someone out with it.

FLO: In the woods along Highway 10, they say there are coyotes.

DARYA: I'm really lucky; my neighbourhood is super safe.

JENNIE: Most of the time, when a guy starts following me and talking to me ...

JOANNE: It doesn't happen to me very often.

KATE: I pretend I'm talking on my phone.

DEZ: I have this mantra: 'Don't fuck with me, don't fuck with me ...'

JOANNE: Sometimes I just burst out running.

ALL: 'Don't fuck with me, don't fuck with me ...'

FLO: But, like, there's no need to be afraid of them. They're more afraid of you than you are of them ...

KATE: They can smell fear.

FLO: The cops are just as bad.

JENNIE: I pretend I'm talking to my boyfriend.

FLO: In Val-d'Ore, if you don't give them a blow job they drive you out of the city and leave you there to freeze.

DEZ: I mean, I guess if they were hungry enough, maybe. You should be careful about being too friendly.

JENNIE: And I say to the pretend boyfriend: 'I'm being followed by this guy who's drunk; I'm on 101st and 95th Street.'

JOANNE: If there's a full moon the park is totally safe.

DARYA: I tell him to fuck off.

DEZ: Sometimes when I'm walking behind a woman and I can tell she doesn't know who's behind her, I make a sound like [*clears throat*].

KATE (*overlapping with Jennie*): One time my English student led me upstairs to write me a cheque, and then blocked the door and trapped me in the bedroom.

JENNIE (*overlapping with Kate*): Once, a cab driver locked the doors and wouldn't let me out until I gave him my number.

DEZ: Or [*sigh*].

DARYA: Sometimes I risk it and sometimes I don't, you know. Sometimes I'm up for it.

KATE: I jumped out through the fire escape.

FLO: I've heard so many stories.

DARYA: My cousin Zahra.

JOANNE: My sister-in-law when she was fourteen.

Extinguishes her light and stops moving.

KATE: My friend Denise.

DEZ: The girl who was murdered in the park by my house.

JOANNE: She tried to scream but no sound came out.

Extinguishes her light and stops.

FLO: Me, when I was in Grade 7.

Extinguishes her light and stops.

JOANNE: After my shift when I was a waitress in Saskatoon.

JENNIE: I'm one of the lucky ones.

Extinguishes her light and stops.

DARYA: On my way home from a gig.

Extinguishes her light and stops.

KATE: On a night train.

JOANNE: Sometimes I just say, *Fuck you! I'm gonna walk where I wanna walk.*

Act 2, Scene 7
Practising

Lights snap up on four women spread around the stage with their backs to the audience. Joanne stands facing the audience next to a chair downstage centre, which was brought on in the darkness. Dez is seated at the piano, Kate stands upstage right, Jennie is on the floor by Joanne's chair, and Darya lays prone upstage left. Throughout this scene, Dez, Kate, Jennie, and Darya pulse their back in varying rhythms, mimicking the beating of Joanne's heart. Joanne takes a few heavy breaths before speaking.

JOANNE: I got this rash all over my face. I went to my doctor and she said, 'Oh, you have seborrheic dermatitis.' And I said, 'What is that?' She said, 'It's from old age and stress.' And I said, 'My daughter's suicidal, my sister has cancer, I have no pension, and the oceans are plastic. So yeah, I'm stressed.'

She felt my pulse, became alarmed, and referred me to a cardiologist. He's calling me with the results today.

So I wait. I'm waiting for a few things. Waiting for my egg to boil. Waiting for it to rain.

Dez starts to fall off the piano bench; Darya gets up and catches her.

Waiting for my newspaper – and the inevitable backlash slash hate mail slash death threats to my last article entitled 'Would The Planet Miss Us, I Think Not.' These days women have named themselves as the saviours of this planet, but we're still driving cars, and renovating our kitchens, and using disposable sanitary products, and saying shitty things about each other on Tweeter. Tooter. Whatever.

Darya exits. Joanne begins to apply lipstick.

Did you know that the average woman will ingest five pounds of lipstick in her lifetime? That's castor oil, beeswax, the smashed little corpses of the South American cochineal beetle, formaldehyde, and lead – so pucker up, ladies.

You might wonder why I'm getting all dolled up. I have a date. (*Laughs.*) No, I do not have a date.

Jennie exits and catches Kate as she is falling on her way out.

I'm practising. I want to look my best at the awards ceremony. Who knows, I might meet a man. This is, however, unlikely. Men who are attracted to sixty-four-year-old women are still with their wives, God bless them.

Kate looks at Joanne. Joanne turns and looks at Kate.

Is that the phone?

Kate looks away, then Joanne looks away.

Sex is complicated. Why I've gone so long without it, I dunno. Too busy, old wounds, no libido – probably because of my radical hysterectomy when I was fifty. Don't let your surgeon tell you that a hysterectomy won't affect your sex life. A novelist I like described the sensation of being inside a woman like me – sand on glass. Nice.

She experiences some pain in her heart, then recovers.

Maybe I'll meet a widower. My mum asked my dad, 'Walter, if I die before you, would you marry again?'

Flo enters, crosses to stage right. She begins to fall and Kate catches her.

He was quiet for a time and then said very gently, 'No, I think I'd just get a dog.' The thought of caring for someone again or making someone breakfast again, or picking someone up at the airport again – it's just so exhausting. I love opening the door to an empty house.

Joanne continues talking, but a Shop-Vac is turned on offstage. The sound takes over and she is not heard.

Act 2, Scene 8
Darya's Veils

Jennie enters stage right with a Shop-Vac, cleaning up the excess blood that has been left onstage. She hears her baby in the audience, offers the vacuum to Joanne, who declines the vacuum and exits. Flo takes over the vacuuming, Jennie cues Kate to take the chair offstage and moves to get her baby from the audience, then walks to the piano bench with a veil covering the baby as she breastfeeds. Darya enters from the aisle and begins her text as she descends through the audience. She is speaking on a handheld microphone.

DARYA: Wavy
Curly
Kinky
Smooth
Cropped
The big chop
Butch
Bob
Bun
Bunches
Bouffant
Chignon
Bettie Page
Finger wave
Fishtail
Ponytail
French twist
Afro
Odango
Cornrows
Dreadlock

Feathered
Fringe
Braid crown
Perm and
Straight
Straight
Straight
Straight, now
Relaxed
Natural
Weave
Full piece
Tracks
Naughty bits, naughty bits, naughty bits, baby doll.

She sits next to Jennie on the piano bench, swinging her legs, then plays piano and sings.

Damn right to hide her head 'cause soon she'll
sprout something that we can't ...

She stops singing and leaves the bench, taking the veil from Jennie's baby.

handle.
It is mental that we have some weird fascination
And disgust.
With not just the tits (*gasp*) the vag or the butt but the
Hair on women's heads
Please, somebody tell me what the deal is and when exactly
that deal was struck
'Cause fuck me if I was ever asked
If I thought grey was a shitty colour.

Walks to centre while changing the veil into various versions of head coverings.

Now his, his history conquers – sorry, concurs –
that we began to veil our women to divide
the shit from the pearls.
Sluts from the girls.

A wimple, a habit,
a mask, a bonnet,
hijab, niqab, paranja –

Off mic, to audience:

Whatever. It sucks to wear a veil if you don't believe in it. Some women choose to, and personally, I can't get behind that, and I know ... that makes me a judgemental asshole. But I grew up believing that hijab was a symbol of oppression, and I would never choose to put a scarf on my head.

Gestures to stage manager booth.

Can you put the thing up?

A photo is projected onto the scrim.

That's me and my dad at a recital in Iran. When I look at this photo, I think: a) I look stupid. Cute, but stupid; b) how do you play violin with all this fabric everywhere, it's hard; and c) thank god – sorry, thank my parents – that they 'got me out of there.' But actually, hijab is the least of the things they saved me from. Women in Tehran are competing with hundreds of thousands of others to get into university, they're worrying about sanctions and the price of bread, they can't breathe from the pollution outside. What's throwing a scarf on your head on your way out the door? They don't have the privilege or the luxury to get up onstage in their bra and underwear and explore the ways women disappear in our society. I do.

On mic:

Cathedral veil, bubble veil, classic bride, modern bride
please continue
go ahead and hide your shame, bitches.
Except in France, no, don't go there
'Cause the po po will strip you on their fancy beaches and
No, no, don't enter the courtroom, boardroom, or golf course
of course cause a bunch of men ...

The rest of the women enter the stage to surround Darya in trench coats that are lined with the bright colours of autumn.

Are still talking 'bout our heads and wombs and force yourself to pray that they are not basing their laws or philosophies on ancient Greece where Aristotle –

Closes her legs.

Amen.
Defined (*Drum*) (*Growl*)
That women are not animals, silly-billy,
We're just sub-men.

Act 3, Scene 1
Fall Dance

The sound of wind and chimes. The fall projection comes up – the title 'FALL' and imagery of a reclining woman, lit by moving autumn light through a window. All women are wearing autumn trench coats that are lined with different bright colours. Kate is on the piano with the vocoder. The others are in a cluster, waiting for something.

All the women onstage move simultaneously, starting with subtle gestures that increase in intensity to take over every body part. It is a movement of resisting gravity, falling, and recovering. At a certain point, words emerge from the vocoder in an affected, digital voice. The text below is spoken and eventually layered, accompanied by synth chords and beats from a recorded track. The music builds until all five women are moving together to a techno anthem. They shed their coats on the floor, revealing their colourful linings, and the movement transforms into a celebratory ecstatic dance. Kate leaves the piano and joins the movement. From the vocoder:

It's getting harder
It's getting harder
It's getting harder to hang on
Everything is falling
It's falling but I'm still hanging on
And now I'm brighter
Yeah I'm the brightest
Motherfucker
You've ever seen now
You've ever seen
still hanging on

It's getting harder
It's getting harder to hang on

Everything is falling
It's falling but I'm still hanging on
And now I'm brighter
Yeah I'm the brightest
Motherfucker
You've ever seen now
You've ever seen
still hanging on

Seems like I
Seems like I never
Seems like I never
Never no never no never ever never could I ever never
Seems Like I Never
See you anymore
Seems Like I Never
See you anymore

Both the first and second set of lyrics are then mixed together.

Act 3, Scene 2
The Fall

Darya breaks out of the dancing cluster. The music continues faintly as though through the wall of a club, while the other women continue the choreography in slow motion. As Darya speaks, she attempts to do a handstand again and again, failing each time but continuing to try.

DARYA: You know what, babies, it is not an accident.

To an audience member:

Um, can you hold this, please?

Gives them the mic.

Thanks, you can sit down.
It is not. By. Accident.
The fall
And it is painful.
To get up another time
One more time
and try it all
again
And again
It is painful
To rage, to sharpen your elbows and dig your way through.
You know what I mean?
It is painful
It is painful
To try
To be seen.

Act 3, Scene 3
Kate's Conference 3

Lights snap up, and Kate abruptly begins her scene. As the rest of the women exit, Darya crosses Kate, who mimes taking a canape from her as if Darya was a server. Joanne moves to the piano and Jennie picks up the discarded autumn coats before exiting. Joanne plays 'The Autumn Leaves' on piano. Kate is left centre stage.

KATE: It's a benefit tonight at the Marriott Hotel, for the donors who funded the expedition. The culinary theme this evening is honey. And I can tell you that they have chosen a pasteurized brand, which is of course totally void of any vitamins or enzymes, and for the life of me I can't tell you why anyone would want to remove the pollen, but anyway. Not all the team is here. We leave in four weeks and everyone's rushing around finalizing visas and equipment and vaccines. I'm already topped up. You've got measles, mumps, diphtheria ...

Sees Daniel to her left.

Oh, Daniel Lovett is at my side. Got some honey-glazed spare ribs. You know who Daniel is, of course – a living legend. Now director-general of the UN's Food and Agriculture Organization –

Daniel interrupts.

Um, no, I don't mind at all, I'm thirty-seven years old, actually ... Yeah, yes. Well, I guess, yep, I can be, yes, classified under the category of a young woman.

Tetanus, of course, hepatitis A, hepatitis B, rubella –

Daniel interrupts.

Oh, wow, well, thank you, Daniel. Yep, uh, I am indeed wearing pants, thank you for noticing.

And, it being Brazil, you've got yellow fever, typhoid, malaria –

Daniel interrupts.

Yeah, no, um, well, I think (*checks back of pants*) Zara ... Zika. (*Beat*) Zika virus. (*Beat*) There's no ... vaccine for Zika virus. Fuck ... fuck.

Flinches, sees Daniel.

Daniel is testing out the depth of one of my trouser pockets. He's still got rib sauce on his fingers ... You know, if I wait, if I don't go to Brazil, then what? What would be the result? Well, they'll go without me, the last four years of my life ... You know my research and my methods will, well, I mean, those guys will be able to finish but, I won't be there, you know, I won't be there at that moment when you find out that that thing you knew, that feeling ...

Touches gut.

... that you know, well, that it's proven to be true. But yeah, I mean, and my name will be there.

Beat. Looks down at her pocket, turns to look at Daniel, then turns out.

But as a footnote.

Flo enters stage left with a chair, Kate stops her and asks, 'What am I going to do?' Flo breaks away and Kate walks forward, crosses to the audience, and goes up to several audience members. She looks in their eyes, touches their arm or hand or shoulder, and asks them, 'What do I do?' 'Tell me, what do you think I should do?' Flo, Joanne, Dez, and Darya continue to set chairs onstage for the Shirt Dance.

Act 3, Scene 4
The Shirt Dance

While Kate is in the audience, Jennie clumsily brings her stroller down the aisle from the top of the audience, saying, 'Sorry, sorry, sorry.' The other women have brought on six chairs and sit in a row along the downstage edge. Jennie works her way across the front row of the audience with the stroller, awkwardly apologizing the whole way. She takes the microphone from the audience member holding it, parks the stroller, with difficulty, and unlocks the car seat. Kate passes in front of her to sit in the nearest empty chair. Jennie awkwardly carries the car seat over the row of seated women and finally finds her seat – 'sorry.' The women have followed her with their gaze the whole time. The sound of an air conditioner begins. They shift their gaze in unison.

They perform the shirt choreography, which is a series of attempts by their left hand to invade their personal space through their T-shirt: under/around/inside, from the neck, from the arm, from below. After every left-handed attempt, the right hand attempts to stop it. They try to stay calm and composed while they are becoming more and more harassed and dishevelled. Eventually Flo, Joanne, Dez, and Jennie exit the stage flustered, leaving Kate and Darya at opposite ends of the chairs.

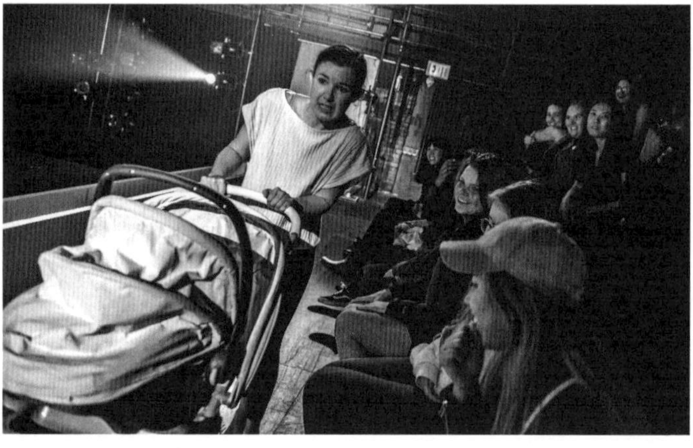

Act 3, Scene 5
Disappearing Act

Darya performs a choreography of climbing over the chairs, each chair becoming the embodiment of woman she speaks about, while Kate sits as though in a doctor's waiting room.

DARYA: Did you know the DNA double helix was discovered
by a woman called Rosalind.
Yeah you know what I'm sayin'.
With two chains and a phosphate backbone, Rosalind
Rewrote biology. For a brace of blokes to break a bond and
steal her notes to publish and press out on paper her break-through
and the Nobel Prize
Is wiped clean and sterilized
of her name.
Split then decay.
Nuclear fission
was borne of a woman named Lise,
not the man Otto Hann who failed to say her name when he
claimed that he split that atom alone.
That atom alone
That adam alone
Won the Nobel in 1944.
Yes, no accident
that Chien-Shiung Wu flipped the law of conservation of
parity on its head, which led to a Nobel for Yang and Lee.
The X and Y chromosomes uncovered by Nettie
but Tom – born with dick and some balls –
got the call from Nobel, same, as well
For Frieda Saur, Candace Pert, and Jocelyn Bell,
It's kinda hard

For me to tell if this is boring you.
A *gaggle of gals* who changed the world for us
That no one ever knew.

Dorothy Vaughan, Angelina Fanny Hesse, Hedy Lamarr –

You know how it goes.
Obliterated from (the big boys club of) history
Bang bang bang bang

Tan Lei, Maryam Mirzakhani, Fern Hunt, Vivienne Malone-Mayes

Darya ends standing on a chair. She looks at Kate as a recording says Kate's name.

VOICE: Katherine Hanson.

KATE: Yes.

Kate moves offstage as if called into a doctor's office.

Act 3, Scene 6
The Hunter

Dez interrupts the end of the scene by running in singing and dancing. She is singing 'Mine Mine Mine' from Disney's Pocahontas *but can't remember all of the words.*

Darya steps off her chair just before Dez tips it over. Darya catches it, and what proceeds during the Pocahontas *song is a dance of Dez pushing over chairs and the women trying to catch them before they hit the floor. As she finishes the song with a flourish, she lands in Dez's spot downstage left.*

Pocahontas. Anybody? What I mean is my first real apartment! When I moved in I was so pumped. But now I look around, and all I see is Michelle's missing stuff. Oh, you didn't hear – she dumped me. She said I didn't get it. That everyday things are so much harder for her. That I don't have to work a part-time job and that my parents are still helping me. She said that I'm privileged and I don't know what it's like.

And here's another picture of her and Chelsea. She's fluent in Cree and she's president of the Indigenous Students' Association. Ugh, she's braiding her hair. Can you believe that?! Rude. I hope she says my name when they fuck.

Lights change and club music comes on.

I'm on the hunt. Got my best outfit on. 'Long hair, don't care.' Some guy's like, 'Hey, where you going?'

Left hand on arm, pulls away.

Fuckin' aggressive. Then I spot her. Category Sub-Prime: The second most attractive girl in a friend group. 'What are you drinking? Looks good.' I can't hear what she's saying. (*Mouthed*) 'Two more of these.'

Music fades out.

It's funny, a year ago hunting meant something totally different. Dad and I went out to the bush and he decided I was finally responsible enough to handle the rifle. (*Hold signal*) I spot the ear of a deer. A two point. Young. But the best meat. I signal to Dad. Try to remember what he taught me. Elbow to the knee, take off the safety, don't put the finger anywhere near the trigger, look through the scope, line up the crosshairs, steady my breath. Aim for its heart. Dad pats me on the back, 'Nice shot, kiddo.' There it is, lifeless. I offer tobacco and give thanks. Honouring the deer.

In the morning I ask for this girl's number out of politeness. Then I do the walk of game. I'm back in my apartment; Michelle's stuff is still missing.

She checks her phone.

Oh my God.

Turns shyly, then does the ecstatic dance from the beginning of the play.

I got three B's AND an A, what?! Am I good at this? I might be good at this.

Darya enters carrying Dez's fur coat, hands it to her, and exits while watching her.

I gotta tell my parents. If I leave right now I can catch the last ferry. Byeeee!

As she yells 'bye' she runs off to exit through the house, her voice trailing as she disappears. We will not see Dez again until winter.

Act 3, Scene 7
Flo's Dressing Room

Kate and Jennie (as stagehands) run on to place a chair and a piano bench in the centre of the stage and then exit. We can hear the last beats of a pop song. Flo enters, the sound swells.

FLO: Yeah, Jimmy! That was AMAZING!!! I know ... I know! Don't worry ... Flo's got this!

The door shuts, sound is cut. She is midway through taking off her outfit (this is a costume change in her dressing room between acts of her concert) when her phone buzzes. She takes the phone and continues to undress.

FLO: (*Into phone*) Je suis en plein milieu d'un concert! Es-tu sérieux? (*Beat*) Mais dis-moi les détails! Qui, quand, où ... c'est trop loin ... oui, of course. T'es certain que c'est pas trop loin? Merci, mon amour. Merci. Bonsoir. (*Small chuckle.*) Bonne journée.

She puts the phone down. Walks around the chair, taking off her pants, her bodysuit, with excitement, then spreads her arms in total joy.

Ten years. After ten years of marriage. Reality has finally sunk in.

Walking downstage in underwear and bra.

My sister thinks I'm crazy. She says there's no way NO WAY that white dude's gonna understand. Well, FUCK HER! YES! He finally gets it. She was wrong and he finally gets it.

The next line is delivered as her underwear comes off. She looks at the audience.

He found us a dentist. My husband found our kids a Black dentist. A Black dentist!!! (*Beat*) My kids. My kids can finally see the full spectrum of what they can be. Athlete, musician, janitor, doctor, engineer, architect, designer, teacher … dentist. Do you know what's so weird? I've been waiting for this day for so long … (*Takes her bra off, sits*) I never really thought it would happen. And (*refers to phone*) HERE IT IS! (*Takes off wig*)

After years of emailing him at two in the morning; hundreds of conversations detailing the minutiae of my experience, hours curating and limiting the interactions with his family, umpteen explanations why I don't want our kids exposed to Black Peter … yet … it was worth it.

Kate enters, also naked, carrying a wig stand.

FLO: I'm gonna know all the music playing in the waiting room! There's going to be pictures of people who look like me on the walls. And landscapes of places my mom calls home. It was worth it.

KATE: (*While putting Flo's underwear on herself*) Being onstage naked, I'm thinking: Is this the right amount of pubic hair to have? Am I leaking right now? And I feel conflicted about showing you my body, since it's the same body you see all the time.

The rest of the women enter with Flo's jazz outfit and proceed to dress her as they speak. Kate and Darya put on her boots and Jennie puts on her new wig. Her bodysuit, skirt, jewellery, etc. Flo stands in the middle of it all, allowing herself to be dressed and keeping her eyes on the audience. The women continue to focus on their tasks, while delivering the following lines in a factual manner.

JOANNE: As a Black woman, I am thinking about how my character is everything my mother told me not to be.

DARYA: As a Black woman, I am worried that you won't get this scene the way I want you to.

JENNIE: As a Black woman, I am ashamed that I didn't realize my naked body would trigger other Black women.

KATE: As a Black woman, my mental health is shattered by being woke.

JOANNE: As the Black woman, I have done a lot of explaining.

JENNIE: As the Black woman, I have felt betrayed and abandoned.

DARYA: As the Black woman, I was very lonely in this process.

JENNIE: As the Black woman, I don't have the luxury of fitting into this palette of bodies.

KATE: As this Black woman, I'm trying to accept that I shouldn't wear my heart on my sleeve.

JENNIE: I want the freedom to wear my heart on my sleeve.

DARYA: I am learning that I don't have that privilege.

JOANNE: As this Black woman, I feel guilty for loving my body and wanting to share that love.

JENNIE: As this Black woman, I am thinking you may feel my musculature is 'extra.'

DARYA: As this Black woman, I am unsure that you will even know what that means.

They've finished dressing her.

FLO: Amsterdam! Are you ready?

Sounds of crowds cheering. As Flo moves to exit the stage, she turns back to address the audience.

ACTRESS: As the Black woman who wrote this scene, I fucking love doing it.

Flo exits. Darya and Kate clear chair and piano bench. Joanne watches Jennie as she struggles to manoeuvre the stroller and microphone. The sound of a roaring amphitheatre audience swells and morphs into a smaller, more polite audience applause. Jennie steps downstage to speak to the audience.

JENNIE: I have to tell you something –

Jennie decides she can't speak and leaves the stage.

Act 3, Scene 8
Joanne's Fall

Joanne steps up to the mic in the centre of the stage. She is alone.

JOANNE: Good evening.

She looks straight at the audience, clears her throat.

Thank you for this lifetime achievement award. The life expectancy of a woman in Canada is eighty-one and I'm sixty-four. Is there a sniper in the house?

My first assignment at twenty-three was for the *Medicine Hat News* in Alberta. I was investigating a fire on the Nikaneet Reserve in southwest Saskatchewan. And, as I sobbed into my twenty-five-cent draft (eat your heart out, Mr. Ford), my boss said to me, 'Joanne, toughen up. There are no answers. Only good questions. That's where you'll find the truth.'

So I've got a couple of questions for you.

First of all, why the fuck is there no money attached to this award? What do you imagine I live on? My life savings from four decades of fifty cents a word?

I gotta say I just about had a heart attack when you gave me this. I mean, I was pretty sure you wished I was dead. No, that's not quite true. I did hear from Jack. Jack, are you here? There you are, Jack called me back. That's right, you said you thought my bomb story had some legs and that maybe I could put a few words together for you on spec.

And I thought, nope I'm not gonna do that. Fuck you, Jack, and fuck you, others – you know who you are. The seven nuclear bombs that are still missing on this planet? Let them be found by accident. And sisters, though one of you is murdered every six days by your intimate partner, I shall swallow. Frack. Hack. Let the clocks roll back.

Kate and Jennie enter and stand on either side of the stage. Kate has a guitar.

Abortion, who needs it. The coal mines – bring 'em on.

Kate and Jennie begin to sing, underscoring Joanne's next words.

Let the pollinators die and the permafrost turn to jelly. Build more casinos. Bottle more water. Bulldoze more habitat. Hate more men. Let the addict overdose. Censor the ministries. Repeal social assistance. Make more money. And, oh yeah, fuck democracy. I no longer protest.

Kate and Jennie stop singing and exit.

So I practised. Three cops were shaking down a Black teenager – I ducked into Pottery Barn. I heard a gunshot in the middle of the night – I took a pill. A bus driver was shaming a mentally ill man – I finished my Sudoku. The polar bear, a hopeless rack of bones – I changed the channel and watched another episode of *The Good Wife*. I thought I was going mad, but I wasn't. I just needed a day or two to see if I could stop loving you. And you know what? I can't. I do love you so. So my next question for you is this:

What should I do for the rest of my life. Read the paper? God, I suffer reading the paper.

My cardiologist tells me my heart needs a rest. So it's your turn now. It's your time. And it's a tricky time. Do I have more blood to give? I do. Do I have words left? I do. But for now, only these four: Lake. Moon. River. Tree. Thank you again for my lifetime achi–

The mic is cut off, Jennie removes it from the stand. Joanne, interrupted, leaves to sit at the piano.

Act 3, Scene 9
Flo's Jazz Solo

Flo's voice enters just as Joanne is cut off. She enters as she speaks in her jazz outfit, holding her mic. She places it in the stand Joanne had been using. Joanne, Kate, and Jennie accompany on piano, upright bass, and snare drum. Throughout this scene, a recording of audience cheering, clapping, and yelling swells until it completely overtakes Flo's voice.

FLO: Arigatō, Tokyo, arigatō! Is that how you say it? *Arigatō*? You know, it has taken me so long to get here and now that I'm here, I gotta tell you ... it really feels like home.

Recording of 'I love you!' shouted from the audience.

I love you too, baby. Now this is the part of the show where we're supposed to bring it down, so let's bring it right down. 'Cause I know THIS is how you like me, THIS is how you love me best, THIS is how you think you can see me and feel me down inside. And sometimes, sometimes I think about leaving you. I do. But we all know I ain't going nowhere, 'cause I got nowhere to run.

So here we go. This is my love letter to you.

Singing:

Never would I ever, never ever could I ever, baby, never would I ever
Stray
Too far away
From you

No never would I even try
If I grew wings

I wouldn't fly
To some place new

'Cause I am yours
For you to have for you to hold
For you I'll bend, for you I'll fold
For you I'll be true.

Act 3, Scene 10
Anorexia

Jennie walks forward from the piano with urgency, cutting through Flo's final moment, and speaks to the audience from a very close proximity. This is the actor speaking now. It is clearly a break from character, a direct address. The crowd cheering cuts off abruptly. The rest of the women exit.

JENNIE: Okay, I'm gonna tell you something, but before I do I gotta say that this body has not produced a baby. But it has seen a bunch of other shit. I remember this specific day, in the hallway of the eating-disorder ward of the University Hospital, when I was waiting to go into the office to have another consultation, or another checkup, with another nutritionist or psychiatrist or whatever ... and this woman walked by and smiled at me. She must have been about sixty or sixty-five but she looked really old. Her bones were all visible, and she was covered in a layer of blonde hair, and her face was like ... hollow. She was so skinny. She was hooked up to an IV tube on one of those metal poles that was force-feeding her, which wasn't weird to see but the difference was this woman wasn't a teenager, she was old. At sixty years old, she shouldn't have to care about that shit. She was at that time in her life when she should get to be free from caring, or thinking about what anyone else thinks of her. I honestly couldn't figure out what the hell was she doing it for. I guess I had always expected that things would just change. I was waiting for the day I would wake up and I just wouldn't care anymore, or I would finally be skinny enough and that would set me free. It was seeing that woman that made me realize that I had to decide to change.

And I did. I've been recovered for over ten years. Recovered. Whatever that means. As if eating is totally uncomplicated now. I skipped a few meals this week to do the scene at the beginning of the play when I'm in my underwear.

But you know what really gets to me is that I do want to have a baby. I want that. But I'm so afraid of being pregnant and gaining weight that I don't know if I can.

I've just kept all of this shit inside and never told anyone. I felt – I feel – so ashamed. But now I'm tired, I can't take care of my story alone anymore. So that's what I'm doing now. I'm asking you to hear my story, to give me a place to put it outside of myself.

She exits downstage right.

Act 4, Interlude
Darya

Darya begins to speak from up on the catwalk in the dark. The lights come up on her.

DARYA: Now that you have seen – I'm up here, folks – NOW that you have seen –

She is interrupted by a tiny white noise blip.

... these women vanish ...

She gestures for a sound cue 'whoosh' but it doesn't happen.

... vanish ...

She again gestures for a sound cue 'whoosh' but it doesn't happen, she looks to the booth, as if to ask, 'What is happening?'

... vanish –

A loud sound of white noise and projection of static enter, cutting her off. Her light goes black.

(*Off mic as she exits*) For fuck's sake!

Act 4. Scene 1
Winter

The sound of wind, strong, cold, blows in with the winter projection – the title 'WINTER' and imagery of a woman's body, nipples hardening from the cold. Women enter in darkness in fur coats and heels to the sound of crunching snow under foot. The winter choreography uses movements of the hunted animal and the aggression of the hunter. It is a herd of deer feeling constant danger, and a group of women feeling the same. Eventually, sensing a threat, the women take off their heels very slowly, terrified, careful not to make a sound. Dez becomes the hunted. She hears a sound and the others flee offstage. Sound of birds scattering, a blinding flash of light directed at the audience. She turns her back. Beat. She removes her fur coat very slowly, revealing its bright-red lining. She leaves it in a pool of light downstage, and walks in a diagonal shaft of light upstage right to exit.

Jennie enters with her laptop and sits upstage right. Flo walks slowly across the stage, dragging her mic and stand. She drops it, loudly, at centre, then walks off.

Darya runs on, and sees the mic on the ground, sees Jennie. Flustered, she starts to speak but every time she opens her mouth, white noise and a projection of static drown her out. After a few tries, she exits.

Act 4, Scene 2
Letter to a Friend

Jennie, sitting at her computer, is midway through writing an email to a friend in Gmail. The words she types are projected on the scrim. The subject heading is 'Checking in!' The news plays quietly from her phone. Already written and projected:

> *Hi Leah, How are you?! Looks like you had a great vacation with the fam from the photos. I'm just writing to check in and say hi.*

She writes:

> I've only been off work for eight months and it already feels like everyone's forgotten my name. (*She deletes the previous sentence.*) It's getting harder.

Deletes. The cursor blinks. Kate enters and sits centre stage. Slowly, she performs her own abortion, pulling the stuffing from her stomach – a rope made of scarves tied together, the same scarf that wrapped the baby, the same scarf that hid her head, the same scarf that Darya dances with and wears in different ways over the show. While this is happening, Jennie is struggling to find the words. She sits back, lies on her back, stares at the screen. Once Kate's action is established, Jennie stands up and starts running on the spot, her gaze fixed intently. She doesn't stop running until the end of the play. Her email continues as she runs.

> I know every mother has gone through this ...

Deletes text.

> A lot of moms have gone through this.

Deletes text.

I love my baby. Of course I do. It's not that, it's ...

Deletes text.

It was my choice.

Pause, garbage-can icon. Kate has removed all the stuffing. She stands, walks across the stage, and bumps into Jennie, who is still running. Jennie says, 'What the fuck?' Kate is startled. Christmas muzak from a waiting room begins to play abruptly. Kate arrives downstage right looking a bit lost. Flo enters and places a chair downstage right for Kate's scene and gently picks up the stuffing that Kate left on the floor. Joanne sits at the piano upstage left.

Act 4, Scene 3
Kate's Send-Off

A cheesy recording of 'Twelve Days of Christmas' is playing. Kate sits on the chair downstage right and takes a moment to speak.

KATE: I'm waiting to be let into Michael's office. Michael Read. As it turns out, we didn't get one of the grants we were counting on and the expedition has been cancelled. Well, hopefully just postponed ... so Mike wanted me to look over some of the numbers once more and, honestly, I do think we should have only included varroa and Nosema absences as predictors in the model, and I'm pretty sure that now he'll agree. But, you know, he's truly been such a mentor to me over these last four years. I really do value his opinion –

A recording of a man's voice comes from offstage – 'Kathy.'

My name is not Kathy. And it's true there is the possibility of creating a multitude of predictor variables for the multiple Nosema species –

The recording comes again, 'Kathy.'

My name is not Kathy. But that would make the lab work much more difficult –

'Kathy.'

The chorus of women sing a harmony recalling the choir of Kate's first scene that slowly crescendos under her text.

And it's likely that the variables would be correlated, anyway, and have the same effect on the response variable, my name is not Kathy, my name is not Kathy, it's not my name. How long have you known me? You've been to my house, I've babysat your children. I hate the name Kathy, you know my name so why don't you say it? My name is not. Fucking. Kathy!

During 'my name is not Kathy,' Kate picks up the chair, raises it above her head, and smashes it. It breaks into several pieces. 'HOW' brings her down to the floor, and as she sings 'LONG,' she crawls backward across the stage toward the piano. The others' voices trail off during 'long' and they walk off. Kate moves the piano bench, picks up an electric guitar, and lies underneath the piano.

A light begins to malfunction downstage right. Darya enters, taking in Kate under the piano and Jennie running. Darya goes to the light and tries to fix it. There is a flash of light and burst of static. The ladder falls from backstage and hits the deck. Darya runs to pick up the ladder and exits.

Act 4, Scene 4
Joanne's Winter

Snow begins to fall. Joanne crosses to centre stage and pulls on soft woolly socks. Jennie continues to run upstage left. We hear the sound of synthetic wind. Joanne performs a beautiful figure-skating solo in her socked feet. Kate accompanies her on distorted electric guitar from under the piano. Soft reverb. Eventually Joanne's dance brings her in close enough proximity to see the fur coat lying on the stage. The guitar becomes more distorted. She looks at it for a moment, beat, and exits upstage right.

Act 4, Scene 5
Final Text

Darya enters, sees the coat, and goes directly to it. It breaks her. She goes mental with sadness and rage. She runs around the stage, not knowing what to do. The rest of the cast do not see or hear her.

DARYA: (*To the coat*) Where is she?

She crosses to Jennie.

Hey! Where is she? Have you seen her?

Jennie doesn't see her.

Where is she? Stop!

Darya grabs and shakes Jennie. She still doesn't see her. She walks toward Kate under the piano. Joanne enters. Darya to Kate:

What are you doing? She's gone!

Kate doesn't see her, she gets up and leaves. A distorted version of the spring vocals begins to play, underscoring and growing through the rest of the scene. Flo enters and sits downstage right, beginning the spring choreography once again. Darya goes to her, and says:

No, no, stop, stand up, we can't go on without her!

Flo does not see her.

No! Can't you hear me?

Darya goes to the trough that has caught the rain from the opening scene. She splashes water on her face.

Wake up! Ah!

Joanne enters and joins the choreography. Darya goes to her.

Stop! Get up – I know you're tired, but we have to do something!

Joanne does not see her. Darya screams to the booth:

Turn that off!

Kate joins the dance, Darya goes to stop her. The violin rain loop from the beginning of the show joins the chaos.

No, stop it! Stop!

Darya grabs Flo's mic from the floor and yells into it, but it is not working.

Stop, stop, I know you can hear me!

Darya drops the mic and runs up the stairs to the booth. She bangs on the booth window.

Hey! Stop! Go back!

Darya runs back to the stage.

(*To cast*) We have to do something. (*To audience*) We have to do something! What are we going to do? What are we going to do?

The rain begins to fall and a distorted, broken version of the SPRING projection begins to play. Darya takes all of this in. She looks at the rain falling, at the audience. Then, defeated, she backs up and slowly lies on the floor, joining the spring choreography. There is nothing left to do.

Dez enters to stand behind her coat as the sound fades. Throughout her text the women stop performing the spring choreography, watch Dez, then stand and leave, one by one.

DEZ: People walk past, you know. *Drunk whore. Sober up.* Eventually the cops come around and debate whether or not to take me to the emergency room. No one attends to me very quickly. The fur coat waits. It's tripped on and kicked to the side. It becomes weathered in the melting snow. Until an elder recognizes the coat for what it is, even in its distressed state. She cleans the coat in water and leaves it outside in the full moon. Her granddaughter comes to visit. The little one admires the coat. The elder shows the child a piece of copper and they sew it into the lining. They build a fire and the coat is burned with medicines as the elder says a prayer. I am brought back to a memory. I'm in the back seat of the truck with my parents, driving down a winding road on Vancouver Island. I can smell the ocean air. And recognize the arbutus trees. Mom and Dad are playing music on full blast. We all sing at the top of our lungs, laughing at our foolish attempts.

Don't you see, this isn't how it ends. This will happen again. You see me now. What will you do tomorrow?

ÍY, ȻNES QENOṈE HÁLE ṮÁ,. U, EUQ ȻNES QENOṈE HÁLE.

It's good to see you all again. I never see you all.

Act 4, Scene 6
The Great Gig in the Sky

Lights out. Beat. A spotlight comes up, revealing Joanne at a keyboard up on a riser behind the scrim. She starts to play the opening chords to Pink Floyd's 'The Great Gig in the Sky.' The women are lit one by one as they join her on their instrument. Kate on guitar, Darya on bass, Flo on organ, Jennie on drums. Spotlight on Dez downstage left. A drum beat leads her into the deep, wailing vocal line of 'The Great Gig in the Sky.' Her voice soars. It is angry and painful and strong. Both Dez and the instruments grow and swell right up to the most intense part of the song. Dez and the rest of the women are suddenly cut and the spotlights snaps to dark – the music is cut short.

Acknowledgements

This play could not have been assembled without the incredible generosity of our colleagues at Why Not Theatre, Nightwood Theatre, and Buddies in Bad Times. Thank you to the Canada Council for the Arts, the Ontario Arts Council, Toronto Arts Council, and the Stoneboat Farm Artist Retreat. Our deepest gratitude to Emilie Monnet, Natasha Mumba, Casey Peet-Paré, Celia Green, Sadie Epstein-Fine, Linda Goyette, Tara Mohan, Kate Amesbury, and Michele Landsberg.

The epigraph is a quote from bell hooks' *Reel to Real: Race, Class, and Sex at the Movies* (Routledge, 2009).

About the Authors

Amy Nostbakken is an award-winning director, writer, performer, and composer. She is co-artistic director of the theatre company Quote Unquote Collective in Toronto and core member of Theatre Ad Infinitum in the UK. She has created and composed numerous productions including *The Big Smoke* (2011), *Ballad of the Burning Star* (2013), *Bucket List* (2016), and *Mouthpiece* (2015) – which she directed, co-wrote, composed, and performed. *Mouthpiece* was published by Coach House Books and Oberon UK, and continues to tour internationally. It has been adapted into a feature film directed by Patricia Rozema.

Norah Sadava is an award-winning director, writer, and performer. She is co-artistic director of the theatre company Quote Unquote Collective in Toronto. Norah has created and performed numerous productions including *Mouthpiece* (Coach House Books), which she co-wrote and has performed internationally for the last four years. *Mouthpiece* continues to be produced internationally and was adapted into a feature film in collaboration with acclaimed Canadian director Patricia Rozema. Norah is currently working on Quote Unquote's next production *Universal Child Care*, set to premiere in 2021. A graduate of the Dell'Arte International School of Physical Theatre in California, Norah teaches theatre for both adults and young people. She lives in Toronto.

A graduate of Concordia University's Interdisciplinary Studies program, **Lisa Karen Cox** has had the pleasure of working for a wide variety of theatre companies (large and not so large) including: Quote Unquote Collective, Why Not Theatre, Spur-of-the-Moment Shakespeare, Headstrong, Dauntless City Theatre, Shakespeare in the Rough, Theatre Smash, Nightwood Theatre,

National Arts Centre, the Stratford Festival of Canada, and the Royal Shakespeare Company. Often playing men and other mythical creatures, Lisa is also a teacher, choreographer, dancer, and director in addition to being an actor and mother. She relishes work that combines music, movement, and heightened language to create rawfully honest performative experiences.

Born in Iran, raised and living in Toronto, **Raha Javanfar** is a multifaceted artist. As lighting designer, she has worked on numerous productions in Toronto. As projections designer, she has toured the world with Tafelmusik over the course of a decade. A multi-instrumentalist, Raha performs regularly as frontwoman and singer/bassist of her blues/R&B band Bad Luck Woman & Her Misfortunes, and as a fiddle player in the Double Cuts, as well as in numerous other bands. Raha has sat on juries for the Dora Awards, FACTOR, and the OAC. She was co-recipient of the Siminovitch Prize, and is an active arts advocate and ambassador for Music Canada.

Cheyenne Scott is Straits Salish of the Saanich Nation and a theatre artist with a focus on developing new Canadian works. Through impactful personal expression and storytelling, her work is an exploration and celebration of her Indigenous heritage. She strives to inform settlers with truth and, more importantly, honour the people of her community by creating vibrant characters that are full of life and hope. Having learned theatre through a colonial process, she is working to indigenize her practice. She is invested in the powerful voice of the youth and supporting their growth.

Maggie Huculak has performed on Canadian stages for forty years. Cherished artistic collaborations include Necessary Angel (with Canadian writers Michael Ondaatje, Colleen Murphy, and John Mighton, and directors Richard Rose and Daniel Brooks), the late great Theatre Columbus (Martha Ross/Leah Cherniak), Soulpepper Theatre, Globe Theatre, and Quote Unquote Collective. She's premiered scores of Canadian writers' plays, and is the co-author of five collective creations: *Mein*, *Hysterica*, *The Betrayal*, *Lonely Nights and Other Stories*, and *Now You See Her*. She has worked extensively in film, television, and radio, and was the sole narrator of the epic CBC documentary series *Canada: A People's History*. Maggie is a six-time Dora Award nominee, and is the recipient of a Dora Award and a Chalmers Award.

Typeset in Albertan and DIN Next Pro.

Printed at the Coach House on bpNichol Lane in Toronto, Ontario, on Zephyr Antique Laid paper, which was manufactured, acid-free, in Saint-Jérôme, Quebec, from second-growth forests. This book was printed with vegetable-based ink on a 1973 Heidelberg KORD offset litho press. Its pages were folded on a Baumfolder, gathered by hand, bound on a Sulby Auto-Minabinda, and trimmed on a Polar single-knife cutter.

Edited by Crystal Sikma and Alana Wilcox
Cover and interior designed by Crystal Sikma
Cover image and final image by Brooke Wedlock
Production stills by Dahlia Katz

Coach House Books
80 bpNichol Lane
Toronto ON M5S 3J4
Canada

416 979 2217
800 367 6360

mail@chbooks.com
www.chbooks.com